The Stages in the Social History of Capitalism

Henri Pirenne

Alpha Editions

This edition published in 2024

ISBN : 9789362092601

Design and Setting By
Alpha Editions
www.alphaedis.com
Email - info@alphaedis.com

As per information held with us this book is in Public Domain.
This book is a reproduction of an important historical work. Alpha Editions uses the best technology to reproduce historical work in the same manner it was first published to preserve its original nature. Any marks or number seen are left intentionally to preserve its true form.

THE STAGES IN THE SOCIAL HISTORY OF CAPITALISM

In the pages that follow I wish only to develop a hypothesis. Perhaps after having read them, the reader will find the evidence insufficient. I do not hesitate to recognize that the scarcity of special studies bearing upon my subject, at least for the period since the end of the Middle Ages, is of a nature to discourage more than one cautious spirit. But, on the one hand, I am convinced that every effort at synthesis, however premature it may seem, cannot fail to react usefully on investigations, provided one offers it in all frankness for what it is. And, on the other hand, the kind reception which the ideas here presented received at the International Congress of Historical Studies held at London last April, and the desire which has been expressed to me by scholars of widely differing tendencies to see them in print, have induced me to publish them. Various objections which have been expressed to me, as well as my own subsequent reflections, have caused me to revise and complete on certain points my London address. In the essential features, however, nothing has been changed.

A word first of all to indicate clearly the point of view which characterizes the study. I shall not enter into the question of the formation of capital itself, that is, of the sum total of the goods employed by their possessor to produce more goods at a profit. It is the capitalist alone, the holder of capital, who will hold our attention. My purpose is simply to characterize, for the various epochs of economic history, the nature of this capitalist and to search for his origin. I have observed, in surveying this history from the beginning of the Middle Ages to our own times, a very interesting phenomenon to which, so it seems to me, attention has not yet been sufficiently called. I believe that, for each period into which our economic history may be divided, there is a distinct and separate class of capitalists. In other words, the group of capitalists of a given epoch does not spring from the capitalist group of the preceding epoch. At every change in economic organization we find a breach of continuity. It is as if the capitalists who have up to that time been active, recognize that they are incapable of adapting, themselves to conditions which are evoked by needs hitherto unknown[2] and which call for methods hitherto unemployed. They withdraw from the struggle and become an aristocracy, which if it again plays a part in the course of affairs, does so in a passive manner only, assuming the rôle of silent partners. In their place arise new men, courageous and enterprising, who boldly permit themselves to be driven by the wind actually blowing and who know how to trim their sails to take advantage of it, until the day comes when, its direction changing and disconcerting their manoeuvres, they in their turn pause and are distanced by new craft having fresh forces and new directions. In short, the permanence throughout the centuries of a capitalist class, the result of a continuous development and changing itself to suit changing circumstances, is not to be affirmed. On the contrary, there are as many classes of capitalists as there are epochs in economic history. That history does not present itself to the eye of the observer under the guise of an inclined plane; it resembles rather a staircase, every step of which rises abruptly above that which precedes it. We do not find ourselves in the presence of a gentle and regular ascent, but of a series of lifts.

In order to establish the validity of these generalizations it is of course needful to control them by the observation of facts, and the longer the period of time covered the more convincing will the observations be. The economic history of antiquity is still too little known, and its relations to the ages which follow have escaped us too completely, for us to take our point of departure there; but the beginning of the Middle Ages gives us access to a body of material sufficient for our purpose.

But first of all, it is needful to meet a serious objection. If it is in fact true, as seems to be usually conceded since the appearance of Bücher's brilliant *Entstehung der Volkswirtschaft*[2]—to say nothing here of the thesis since formulated with such extreme radicalism by W. Sombart[3]—that the economic organisation of the Middle Ages has no aspect to which one can rightly apply the term capitalistic, then our thesis is limited wholly to modern times and there can be no thought of introducing into the discussion the centuries preceding the Renaissance. But whatever may be the favor which it still enjoys, the theory which refuses to perceive in the medieval urban economy the least trace of capitalism has found in recent times ever increasing opposition. I will not even enumerate here the studies which seem to me to have in an incontrovertible manner established the fact that all the essential features of capitalism—individual enterprise, advances on credit, commercial profits, [3]speculation, etc.—are to be found from the twelfth century on, in the city republics of Italy—Venice,[4] Genoa,[5] or Florence.[6] I shall not ask what one can call such a navigator as Romano Mairano (1152-1201), if, in spite of the hundreds of thousands of francs he employed in business, the fifty per cent. profits he realized on his operations in coasting trade, and his final failure, one persists in refusing to him the name of capitalist. I shall pass over the disproof of the alleged ignorance of the medieval merchants. I shall say nothing of the astonishing errors committed in the calculations, so confidently offered to us as furnishing mathematical proof of the naïveté of historians who can believe the commerce of the thirteenth and fourteenth centuries to have been anything more than that of simple peddlers, a sort of artisans incapable of rising even to the idea of profit, and having no views beyond the day's livelihood.[7] Important as all this may be, the weak point in the theory which I am here opposing seems to me to lie especially in a question of method. Bücher and his partizans, in my opinion, have, without sufficient care, used for their picture of the city economy of the Middle Ages the characteristics of the German towns and more particularly the German towns of the fourteenth and fifteenth centuries. Now the great majority of the German towns of that period were far from having attained the degree of development which had been reached by the great communes of northern Italy, of Tuscany, or of the Low Countries. Instead of presenting the classical type of urban economy, they are merely examples of it incompletely developed; they present only certain manifestations; they lack others, and particularly those which belong to the domain of capitalism. Therefore in presenting as true of all the cities of the Middle Ages a theory which rests only on the observation of certain of them, and those the least advanced, one is necessarily doing violence to reality. Bücher's description of *Stadtwirtschaft* remains a masterpiece of penetration and economic understanding. But it is too restricted. It does not take account of certain elements of the problem, because these elements were not encountered in the narrow circle which the research covered. One may be confident that if, instead of proceeding from the analysis of such towns as Frankfort, this study had[4] considered Florence, Genoa, and Venice, or even Ghent, Bruges, Ypres, Douai, or Tournai, the picture which it furnished us would have been very different. Instead of refusing to see capitalism of any kind in the economic life of the bourgeoisie, the author would have recognized, on the contrary, unmistakable evidences of capitalism. I shall later have occasion to return to this very essential question. But it was indispensable to indicate here the position which I shall take in regard to it.

Of course I do not at all intend to reject *en bloc* the ideas generally agreed upon concerning the urban economy of the Middle Ages. On the contrary, I believe them to be entirely accurate in their essential elements, and I am persuaded that, in a very large number of cases, I will even say, if you like, in the majority of cases, they provide us with a theory which is completely satisfactory. I am very far from maintaining that capitalism exercised a preponderant influence on the character of economic organization from the twelfth to the fifteenth centuries. I believe that, though it is not right to call this organization "acapitalistic", it is on the other hand correct to consider it "anticapitalistic". But to affirm this is to affirm the existence of capital. That organization recognized the existence of capital since it tried to defend itself against it, since, from the end of the thirteenth century onward, it took more and more measures to escape from its abuses. It is incontestable that, from this period on, it succeeded by legal force in diminishing the rôle which capitalism had played up to that time. In fact it is certain, and we shall have occasion to observe it, that the power of capital was much greater during the first part of the urban period of the Middle Ages than during the second. But even in the course of the latter period, if municipal legislation seems more or less completely to have shut it out from local markets, capital succeeded in preserving and in dominating a very considerable portion of economic activity. It is capital which rules in inter-local commerce, which determines the forms of credit, and which, fastening itself on all the industries which produce not for the city market but for exportation, hinders them from being controlled, as the others are, by the minute regulations which in innumerable ways cramp the activity of the craftsmen.[8]

Let us recognize, then, that capitalism is much older than we have ordinarily thought it. No doubt its operation in modern times has been much more engrossing than in the Middle Ages. But that is only a difference of quantity, not a difference of quality, a simple difference of intensity not a difference of nature. Therefore, we[9] are justified in setting the question we set at the beginning. We can, without fear of pursuing a vain shadow, endeavor to discern what throughout history have been the successive stages in the social evolution of capitalism.

Of the period which preceded the formation of towns, that is, of the period preceding the middle of the eleventh century, we know too little to permit ourselves to tarry there. What may still have survived in Italy and in Gaul of the economic system of the Romans has disappeared before the beginning of the eighth century. Civilization has become strictly agricultural and the domain system has impressed its form upon it. The land, concentrated in large holdings in the hands of a powerful landed aristocracy, barely produces what is necessary for the proprietor and his *familia*. Its harvests do not form material for commerce. If during years of exceptional abundance the surplus is transported to districts where scarcity prevails, that is all. In addition certain commodities of ordinary quick consumption, and which nature has distributed unequally over the soil, such as wine or salt, sustain a sort of traffic. Finally, but more rarely, products manufactured by the rural industry of countries abounding in raw materials, such as, to cite only one, the friezes woven by the peasants of Flanders, maintain a feeble exportation. Of the condition of the *negociatores* who served as the instruments of these exchanges, we know almost nothing. Many of them were unquestionably merchants of occasion, men without a country, ready to seize on any means of existence that came their way. Pursuers of adventure were frequent among these roving creatures, half traders, half pirates, not unlike the Arab merchants who even to our day have searched for and frequently have found fortunes amid the negro populations of Africa. At least, to read the history of that Samo who at the beginning of the eighth century, arriving at the head of a band of adventuring merchants among the Wends of the Elbe, ended by becoming their king, makes one think involuntarily of certain of those beys or sheiks encountered by voyagers to the Congo or the Katanga.[9] Clearly no one will try to find in this strong and fortunate bandit an ancestor of the capitalists of the future. Commerce, as he understood and practised it, blended with plunder, and if he loved gain it was not in the manner of a man of affairs but rather in that of a primitive conqueror with whom violence of appetite took the place of calculation. Samo was evidently an exception. But the spirit which inspired him may have inspired a goodly number of *negociatores* who[6] launched their barks on the streams of the ninth century. In the society of this period only the possession of land or attachment to the following of a great man could give one a normal position. Men not so provided were outside the regular classification, forming a confused mass, in which were promiscuously mingled professional beggars, mercenaries in search of employment, masters of barges or drivers of wagons, peddlers, traders, all jostling in the same sort of hazardous and precarious life, and all no doubt passing easily from one employment to another. This is not to say, however, that among the *negociatores* of the Frankish epoch there were not also individuals whose situation was more stable and whose means of existence were less open to suspicion. Indeed, we know that the great proprietors, lay or ecclesiastical, employed certain of their serfs or of their *ministeriales* in a sporadic commerce of which we have already mentioned above the principal features. They commissioned them to buy at neighboring markets the necessary commodities or to transport to places of sale the occasional surplus of their grain or their wine. Here too we discover no trace of capitalism. We merely find ourselves in the presence of hereditary servants performing gratuitous service, entirely analogous to military service.

Nevertheless commercial intercourse produced even then, in certain places particularly favored by their geographic situation, groups of some importance. We find them along the sea-coast—Marseilles, Rouen, Quentovic—or on the banks of the rivers, especially in those places where a Roman road crosses the stream, as at Maastricht on the Meuse or at Valenciennes on the Scheldt. We are to think of these *portus* as wharves for merchandise and as winter quarters for boats and boatmen. They differ very distinctly from the towns of the following period. No walls surround them; the buildings which are springing up seem to be scarcely more than wooden sheds, and the population which is found there is a floating population, destitute of all privileges and forming a striking contrast to the bourgeoisie of the future. No organization seems to have bound together the adventurers and the voyagers of these *portus*. Doubtless it is possible, it is even probable, that a certain number of individuals, profiting by circumstance, may have little by little devoted themselves to trade in a regular fashion and have begun by the ninth century to form the nucleus of a group of professional traders. But we have too little information to enable us to speak with any precision.

The operations of credit follow much the same course. We cannot doubt that loans had been employed in the Carolingian period, and the Church as well as the State had occupied itself in combating[7] their abuses.[10] But it would be a manifest exaggeration to deduce from this the existence of even a rudimentary capitalistic economy. Everything indicates that the loans which we are considering here were only occasional loans, of usurious nature, to which people who had met with some catastrophe, such as war, a fire, or a poor harvest, were forced to have recourse temporarily.

Thus, the early centuries of the Middle Ages seem to have been completely ignorant of the power of capital. They abound in wealthy landed proprietors, in rich monasteries, and we come upon hundreds of sanctuaries the treasure of which, supplied by the generosity of the nobles or the offerings of the faithful, crowds the altar with ornaments of gold or of solid silver. A considerable fortune is accumulated in the Church, but it is an idle fortune. The revenues which the landowners collect from their serfs or from their tenants are directed toward no economic purpose. They are scattered in alms, in the building of monuments, in the purchase of works of art, or of precious objects which should serve to increase the splendor of religious ceremonies. Wealth, capital, if one may so term it, is fixed motionless in the hands of an aristocracy, priestly or military. This is the essential condition of the patronage that this aristocracy (*majores et divites*) exercises over the people (*pauperes*). Its action is as important from the social point of view as it is unimportant from that of economics. No part of it is directed toward the *negociatores*, who, left to themselves, live, so to speak, on the fringe of society. And so it will continue to be, for long centuries.

Landed property, indeed, did not contribute at all to that awakening of commercial activity which, after the disasters of the Norman invasion in the North and the Saracen raids on the shores of the Mediterranean, began to manifest itself toward the end of the tenth century and the beginning of the eleventh. Its preliminary manifestations are found at the two extremities of the Continent, Italy and the Low Countries. The interior seas, between which Europe was restricted in her advance toward the Atlantic, were its first centres of activity. Venice, then Genoa and Pisa, venture on the coasting trade along their shores, and then maintain, with their rich neighbors of Byzantium or of the Mohammedan countries, a traffic which henceforward constantly increases. Meanwhile Bruges at the head of the estuary of the Zwyn, becomes the centre of a navigation[8] radiating toward

England, the shores of North Germany, and the Scandinavian regions. Thus, economic life, as in the beginning of Hellenic times, first becomes active along the coasts. But soon it penetrates into the interior of the country. Step by step it wins its way along the rivers and the natural routes. On this side and on that, it arouses the hinterland into which the harbors cut their indentations. In this process of growth the two movements finally meet, and bring into communication the people of the North and the people of the South. By the beginning of the twelfth century it is an accomplished fact. In 1127 Lombard merchants, journeying by the long route which descends from the passes of the Alps toward Champagne and the Low Countries, reach the fairs of Flanders.

If the feeble and precarious commercial activity of the Carolingian period was sufficient to create gathering-places of merchants at the points most frequented in travel, it is not difficult to understand that the steady progress of economic activity from the end of the tenth century would result in the formation, at the strategic points of regional transit, of aggregations of like character but much more important and more stable. The surface of the land, the direction and the depth of the streams, determining the routes of commerce, also determined the location of the towns. Indeed, European cities are the daughters of commerce and of industry. Unquestionably in the countries of old civilization, in Italy or in Gaul, the Roman cities had not completely disappeared. Within the circle of their walls, which had now become too large and were filled with ruins, there gathered, around the bishop resident in each of them, a whole population of clerics and monks, and beside them a lay population employed in their service or support. In the North, one found the same spectacle at the centres of the new dioceses, at Thérouanne, at Utrecht, at Magdeburg, or at Vienna. But here was no trace, properly speaking, of municipal life. A certain number of artisans, some of them serfs, a little weekly market for the most indispensable commodities, sometimes a fair visited by the merchant-adventurers of whom we have spoken above—this is the sum total of economic life.

But the situation changes from the moment when the increasing intensity of commerce begins to furnish men with new means of existence. Immediately one discovers an uninterrupted movement of migration of peasants from the country towards the places in which the handling of merchandise, the towing of boats, the service of merchants furnish regular occupations and arouse the hope of gain.

If the old cities disadvantageously placed at one side from the highways of travel continue in their torpor, the others see their[9] population increase continuously. Suburbs join the old enclosure; new markets are established; new churches are built for the new comers; and soon the primitive nucleus of the town, surrounded on all sides by the houses of the immigrants, becomes merely the quarter of the priests, bound to the shadow of the cathedral and submerged on all sides by the expansion of lay life. Much that at the beginning was the essential is now nothing more than the accessory. The episcopal burg disappears amid faubourgs.[11] The city has not been formed by growing with its own forces. It has been brought into existence by the attraction which it has exerted upon its surroundings whenever it has been aided by its situation. It is the creation of those who have migrated toward it. It has been made from without and not from within. The bourgeoisie of the oldest towns of Europe is a population of the transplanted. But it is at the same time essentially a trading population, and no other proof of this need be advanced than the fact that, down to the beginning of the twelfth century, *mercator* and *burgensis* were synonymous terms.

Whence came these pioneers of commerce, these immigrants seeking means of subsistence, and what resources did they bring with them into the rising towns? Doubtless only the strength of their arms, the force of their wills, the clearness of their intelligence. Agricultural life continued to be the normal life and none of those who remained upon the soil could entertain the idea of abandoning his holding to go to the town and take his chances in a new existence. As for selling the holding to get ready money, like the men of a modern rural population, no one at that time could have imagined such a transaction. The ancestors of the bourgeoisie must then be sought, specifically, in the mass of those wandering beings who, having no land to cultivate, floated across the surface of society, living from day to day upon the alms of the monasteries, hiring themselves to the cultivators of the soil in harvest time, enlisting in the armies in time of war, and shrinking from neither pillage nor rapine if the occasion presented itself. It may without difficulty be admitted that there may have been among them some rural artisans or some professional peddlers. But it is beyond question that with very few exceptions it was poor men who floated to the towns and there built up the first fortunes in movable property that the Middle Ages knew.

[10]

Fortunately we possess certain narratives which enable us to support this thesis with concrete examples. It will suffice to cite here the most characteristic of them, the biography of St. Godric of Finchale.[12]

He was born of poor peasants in Lincolnshire, toward the end of the eleventh century, and from infancy was forced to tax his ingenuity to find the means of livelihood. Like many other unfortunates of all times, he at first walked the beaches on the outlook for wreckage cast up by the sea. Then we see him, perhaps by reason of some fortunate find, setting up as a peddler and travelling through the country with a little pack of goods (*cum mercibus minutis*). At length he gathers together a small sum, and one fine day joins a troop of town merchants whom he has met in the course of his wanderings. Thenceforward he goes with his companions from market to market, from fair to fair, from town to town. Having thus become a professional merchant, he rapidly gains a sufficient sum to enable him to associate himself with other merchants, charter a boat with them, and engage in the coasting trade along the shores of England, Scotland, Denmark, and Flanders. The company is highly successful. Its operations consist in carrying to a foreign country goods which it knows to be uncommon there, in selling them there at a high price, and acquiring in exchange various merchandise which it takes pains to dispose of in the places where the demand for them is greatest and where it can consequently make the greatest gains. At the end of some years this prudent practice of buying cheap and selling dear has made of Godric, and doubtless of his associates, a man of important wealth. Then, touched by divine grace, he suddenly renounces his fortune, gives his goods to the poor, and becomes a monk.

The story of Godric, if one omits its pious conclusion, must have been that of many others. It shows us, with perfect clearness, how a man beginning with nothing might in a relatively short time amass a considerable capital. Our adventurer must have been favored by circumstances and chance. But the secret of his success, and the contemporary biographer to whom we owe the story insists strongly upon it, is intelligence.[13] Godric in fact shows himself a calculator, I might even say a speculator. He has in a high degree the feeling, and it is much more developed among minds without culture than is usually thought, for what is practicable in commerce. He is on fire[11] with the love of gain. One sees clearly in him that famous *spiritus capitalisticus* of which some would have us believe that it dates only from the time of the Renaissance. Here is an eleventh-century merchant, associated with companions like himself, combining his purchases, reckoning his profits, and, instead of hiding in a chest the money he has gained, using it only to support and extend his business. More than this, he does not hesitate to devote himself to operations which the Church condemns. He is not disquieted by the theory of the just price; the Decretum of Gratian disapproves in express terms of the speculations which he practises: "Qui comparat rem ut illam ipsam integram et immutatam dando lucretur, ille est mercator qui de templo Dei ejicitur".

After this, how can we see, in Godric and any of those who led the same sort of life, anything else but capitalists? It is impossible to maintain that these men conducted business only to supply their daily wants, impossible not to see that their purpose is the constant accumulation of goods, impossible to deny that, barbarous as we may suppose them, they none the less possessed the comprehension, or, if one prefers, had the instinct for commerce on the large scale.[14] Of the organization of this commerce the life of Godric shows us already the principal features, and the description which it gives us of them is the more deserving of confidence because it is corroborated in the most convincing fashion by many documents. It shows us, first of all, the merchant coming from the country to establish himself in the town. But the town is to him, so to speak, merely a basis of operations. He lives there but little, save in the winter. As soon as the roads are practicable and the sea open to navigation, he sets out. His commerce is essentially a wandering commerce, and at the same time a collective one, for the insecurity of the roads and the powerlessness of the solitary individual compel him to have recourse to association. Grouped in gilds, in hanses, in *caritates*, the associates take their merchandise in convoy from town to town, presenting a spectacle entirely like that which the caravans of the East still furnish in our day. They buy and sell in common, dividing the profits in the ratio of their respective investments in the expedition, and the trade they carry on in the foreign markets is wholesale trade, and can only be that, for retail trade, as the life of Godric shows us, is left to the rural peddlers. It is in gross that they export and import wine, grain, wool, or cloth. To convince ourselves of this we need only examine the regulations which have been[12] preserved to us. The statutes of the Flemish hanse of London, for example, formally exclude retail dealers and craftsmen from the company.

Moreover, the merchant associations of the eleventh and twelfth centuries have nothing exclusively local in their character. In them we find bourgeoisie of different towns, side by side. They have rather the appearance of regional than of urban organisms. They are still far from the exclusivism and the protectionism which are to be shown with so much emphasis in the municipal life of the fourteenth century. Commercial freedom is not troubled by any restrictive regulations. Public authority assigns no limits to the activity of the merchants, does not restrict them to this or that kind of business, exercises no supervision over their operations. Provided they pay the fiscal dues (*teloneum, conductus*, etc.) levied by the territorial prince and the seigneurs having jurisdiction at the passage of the bridges, along the roads and rivers, or at the markets, they are entirely free from all legal obstacles. The only restrictions which hinder the full expansion of commerce do not come from the official authority, but result from the practices of commerce itself. To wit, the various merchant associations, gilds, hanses, etc., which encounter each other at the places of buying and selling, oppose each other in brutal competition. Each of them excludes from all participation in its affairs the members of all the others. But this is merely a state of facts, resting on no legal title. Force holds here the place of law, and whatever may be the differences of time and of environment, one cannot do otherwise than to compare the commerce of the eleventh and twelfth centuries to that bloody competition in which, in the sixteenth and seventeenth centuries, the sailors of Holland, England, France, and Spain engaged in the markets of the New World. We shall conclude then that medieval commerce, at its origin, is essentially characterized by its regional quality and by its freedom. And it is not difficult to understand that it was so, if one bears in mind two facts to which attention should be drawn.

In the first place, down to the end of the twelfth century, the number of towns properly so-called was relatively small. Only those places that were favored by a privileged geographical situation attracted the merchants in sufficient number to enable them to maintain a commercial movement of real importance. After that the attraction which these centres of business exerted upon their environs was much greater than is ordinarily imagined. All the secondary localities were subject to their influence. The merchants dwelling in these last, too few to act by themselves, affiliated themselves to the hanse or gild of the principal town. The Flemish[13] hanse, which we have already instanced, proves this fully, by showing us the merchants of Dixmude, Damme, Oudenbourg, Ardenbourg, etc., seeking admission into the hanse of Bruges.

In the second place, at the period we have now reached the towns devoted themselves far more to commerce than to industry. Few could be cited that appear thus early as manufacturing centres. The concentration of artisans within their walls is still incomplete. If their merchants export, along with the products of the soil, such as wine and grain, a quantity of manufactured products, such, for example, as cloth, it is more than probable that these were for the most part made in the country.

Admit these two statements, and the nature of early commerce is explained without difficulty. They account in fact both for the freedom of the merchants and for that character of wholesale exporters which they exhibit so clearly and which prevents our placing them in the category in which the theory of urban economy claims to confine them. Contrary to the general belief, it appears then that before the thirteenth century we find a period of free capitalistic expansion. No doubt the capitalism of that time is a collective capitalism: groups, not isolated individuals, are its instruments. No doubt too it contents itself with very simple operations. The commercial expeditions upon which its activity especially centres itself demand, for their successful conduct, an endurance, a physical strength, which the more advanced stages of economic evolution will not require. But they demand nothing more. Without the ability to plan and combine they would remain sterile. And so we can see that, from the beginning, what we find at the basis of capitalism is intelligence, that same intelligence which Georg Hansen has so well shown, long ago, to be the efficient cause of the emergence of the bourgeoisie.[15]

The fortunes acquired inn the wandering commerce by the parvenus of the eleventh and twelfth centuries soon transformed them into landed proprietors. They invest a good part of their gains in lands, and the land they thus acquire is naturally that of the towns in which they reside. From the beginning of the thirteenth century one sees this land held in large parcels by an aristocracy of patricians, *viri hereditarii, divites, majores,* in whom we cannot fail to recognize the descendants of the bold voyagers of the gilds and the hanses. The continuous increase of the burghal population enriches them more and more, for as new inhabitants establish themselves in the towns, and as the number of the houses increases, the rent of the ground increases in proportion. So, from the commencement[14] of the thirteenth century, the grandsons of the primitive merchants abandon commerce and content themselves with living comfortably upon the revenue of their lands. They bid farewell to the agitations and the chances of the wandering life. They live henceforward in their stone houses, whose battlements and towers rise above the thatched roofs of the wooden houses of their tenants. They assume control of the municipal administration; they and their families monopolize the seats in the *échevinage* or the town council. Some even, by fortunate marriages, ally themselves with the lesser nobility and begin to model their manner of living upon that of the knights.

But while these first generations of capitalists are retiring from commerce and rooting themselves in the soil, important changes are going on in the economic organization. In the first place, in proportion as the wealth of the towns increases, and with it their attractive power, they take on more and more an industrial character, the rural artisans flocking into them *en masse* and deserting the country. At the same time, many of them, favored by the abundance of raw material furnished by the surrounding region, begin to devote themselves to certain specialties of manufacture—cloth-making or metallurgy. Finally, around the principal aggregations many secondary localities develop, so that all Western Europe, in the course of the thirteenth century, blossoms forth in an abundance of large and small towns. Some, and much the greater number of them, content themselves perforce with local commerce. Their production is determined by the needs of their population and that of the environs which extend two or three leagues around their walls and, in exchange for the manufactured articles which the city furnishes to them, attend to the food supply of the urban inhabitants. Other towns, on the contrary, less closely set together but also more powerful, develop chiefly by means of an export industry, producing, as did the cloth industry of great Flemish or Italian cities, not for their local market,[16] but for the European market, constantly extensible. Others still, profiting by the advantages of nearness to the sea, give themselves up to navigation and to transportation, as did so many ports of Italy, of France, of England, and especially of North Germany.

Of these two types of towns, the one sufficient to themselves, the other living upon the outside world, it is unquestionably the first to which the theory of the urban economy applies. Direct trade[15] between purchaser and consumer, strict protectionism excluding the foreigner from the local market and reserving it to the bourgeoisie alone, minute regulations confining within narrow limits the industry of the merchant and the artisan; in a word, all the traits of an organization evidently designed to preserve and safeguard the various members of the community by assigning to each his place and his rôle, are all found and all explained without difficulty in those towns which are confined to a clientage limited by the extent of their suburban dependencies. In these one can rightly speak of an anti-capitalistic economy. In these we find neither great *entrepreneurs* nor great merchants. It is true that the necessity of stocking the town with commodities which it does not produce or cannot find in its environs—groceries, fine cloths, wines in northern countries—brings into existence a group of exporters whose condition is superior to that of their fellow-citizens. But on inspection they cannot be regarded as a class of great professional merchants. If they buy at wholesale in foreign markets, it is to sell at retail to their fellow-citizens. They dispose of their goods piecemeal, and like the *Gewandschneider* of the German towns, they do not rise above the level of large shopkeepers.[17]

In the towns of the second category we find a quite different condition. Here capitalism not only exists but develops toward perfection. Instruments of credit, such as the *lettre de foire*, make their appearance; a traffic in money takes its place alongside the traffic in merchandise and, despite the prohibition of loans at interest, makes constantly more rapid progress. The *coutumes* of the fairs, especially those of the fairs of the Champagne, in which the merchants of the regions most advanced in an economic sense, Italy and the Low Countries, meet each other, give rise to a veritable commercial law. The circulation of money expands and becomes regulated; the coinage of gold, abandoned since the Merovingian period, is resumed in the middle of the thirteenth century. The security of travellers increases on the great highways. The old Roman bridges are rebuilt and here and there canals are built and dykes constructed. Finally, in the towns, the commercial buildings of the previous period, outgrown, are replaced by structures more vast and more luxurious, of which the *halles* of Ypres, with their façade one hundred and thirty-three metres long, is doubtless the most imposing specimen.

In the presence of these facts it is impossible to deny the existence of a considerable traffic. Moreover documents abound which[16] attest the existence in the great cities of men of affairs who hold the most extended relations with the outside world, who export and import sacks of wool, bales of cloth, tuns of wine, by the hundred, who have under their orders a whole corps of factors or "sergents" (*servientes, valets*, etc.), whose letters of credit are negotiated in the fairs of Champagne, and who make loans amounting to several thousands of livres to princes, monasteries, and cities in need of money. To cite here merely a few figures, let us recall that in 1273 the company of the Scotti of Piacenza exports wool from England to the value of 21,400 pounds sterling, or 1,600,000 francs (metallic value);[18] in 1254 certain burgesses of Arras furnish 20,000 livres to the Count of Guines, prisoner of the Count of Flanders, to enable him to pay his ransom.[19] In 1339 three merchants of Mechlin advance 54,000 florins (700,000 francs) to King Edward III.[20]

Extensive however as capitalistic commerce has been since the first half of the thirteenth century, it no longer enjoys the freedom of development which it had before. As we advance toward the end of the Middle Ages, indeed, we see it subjected to limitations constantly more numerous and more confining. Henceforth, in fact, it has to reckon with municipal legislation. Every town now shelters itself behind the ramparts of protectionism. If the most powerful cities can no longer exclude the stranger, upon whom they live, they impose upon him a minute regulation, the purpose of which is to defend against him the position of their own citizens. They force him to have recourse in his purchases to the mediation of his "hosts" and his "courtiers"; they forbid him to bring in manufactured articles which may compete with those which the city produces; they exploit him by levying taxes of all sorts: duties upon weighing, upon measuring, upon egress, etc.

In those cities especially in which has occurred the popular revolution transferring power from the hands of the patriciate into those of the craft-gilds, distrust of capital is carried as far as it can go without entirely destroying urban industry. The craftsmen who produce for exportation—for example, the weavers and the fullers of the towns of Flanders—try to escape from their subjection, to the merchants who employ them. Not only do the municipal statutes fix wages and regulate the conditions of work, but they also limit the independence of the merchant, even in purely commercial matters. It will be sufficient to mention here, as one of their most[17] characteristic provisions, the forbidding of the cloth merchant to be at the same time a wool merchant, a prohibition inspired by the desire to prevent operations that will unfavorably affect prices and the workman's wages.[21]

But it is not solely the municipal authority which attacks the speculations born of the capitalistic spirit. The Church steps forward, and under the name of usury forbids indiscriminately the lending of money at interest, sales on credit, monopolies, and in general all profits exceeding the *justum pretium*. No doubt these prohibitions themselves attest the existence of the abuses which they endeavor to oppose, and their frequency proves that they did not always succeed. It is none the less true that they were very burdensome and that the pursuit of business on a large scale found itself much embarrassed by them.

The increasing specialization of commerce embarrassed it much more. At the beginning the merchants had devoted themselves to the most various operations at once. Wandering from market to market, they bought and sold without feeling in need of centring their activity on this or that kind of products or commodities, but from about 1250 this is no longer the case. The progress of economic evolution has resulted in localizing certain industries and in restraining certain branches of commerce to the groups of merchants best suited to their promotion. Thus, for example, in the course of the thirteenth century the trade in fine cloth became a monopoly of the towns of Flanders, and banking a monopoly of certain merchant companies of Lombardy, Provence, or Tuscany. Thenceforward commercial life ceases to overflow at random, so to speak. It has a less arbitrary, a more deliberate, and consequently a more embarrassed quality.

These limitations resting upon commerce have resulted in turning away from it the patricians, who moreover have become, as has been said above, a class of landed proprietors. The place which they left vacant is filled by new men, among whom, as among their predecessors, intelligence is the essential instrument of fortune. The intellectual faculties which the first developed in wandering commerce are used by these later men to overcome the obstacles raised in their pathway by municipal regulations of commerce and ecclesiastical regulations in respect to money affairs.[22] Many of them find a rich source of profit by devoting themselves to brokerage. Others[18] in the industrial cities exploit shamelessly and in defiance of the statutes the artisans whom they employ. At Douai, for example, Jehan Boinebroke (1280-1310) succeeds in reducing to serfdom a number of workers (and characteristically, they are chiefly women) by advancing wool or money which they are unable to repay, and which therefore place them at his mercy.[23] The richest or the boldest profit by the constantly increasing need of money on the part of territorial princes and kings, to become their bankers. It will be remembered that it was Lombard capitalists who furnished Edward III. with money to prepare his campaigns against France,[24] and, quite recently, the history of Guillaume Servat of Cahors (1280-1320) has shown us a man who, setting out with nothing, like Godric in the eleventh century, accumulates in a few years a considerable fortune, supplies the King of England with a dowry for one of his daughters, lends money to the King of Norway, farms the wool duties at London, and, unscrupulous as he is shrewd, does not hesitate to engage in shady speculations upon the coinage.[25] And how many other financiers do we not know whose career is wholly similar: Thomas Fin at the court of the counts of Flanders,[26] the Berniers at that of the counts of Hainaut, the Tote Guis, the Vane Guis, at that of the kings of France, not to name the numberless Italians entrusted by the popes with the various operations of pontifical finance, those *mercatores Romanam curiam sequentes* among whom are found the ancestors of the great Medici of the fifteenth century.[27]

In the course of the fifteenth century this second class of capitalists, courtiers, merchants, and financiers, successors to the capitalists of the hanses and the gilds, is in its turn drawn along toward the downward grade. The progress of navigation, the discoveries made by the Portuguese, then by the Spaniards, the formation of great monarchical states struggling for supremacy, begin to destroy the economic situation in the midst of which that class had grown to[19] greatness, and to which it had adapted itself. The direction of the currents of commerce is altered. In the north, the English and Dutch marine gradually take the place of the hanses. In the Mediterranean, commerce centres itself at Venice and at Genoa. On the shores of the Atlantic, Lisbon becomes the great market for spices, and Antwerp, supplanting Bruges, becomes the rendezvous of European commerce. The sixteenth century sees this movement grow more rapid. It is favored at once by moral, political, and economic causes; the intellectual progress of the Renaissance, the expansion of individualism, great wars exciting speculation, the disturbance of monetary circulation caused by the influx of precious metals from the New World. As the science of the Middle Ages disappears and the humanist takes the place of the scholastic, so a new economy rises in the place of the old urban economy. The state subjects the towns to its superior power. It restrains their political autonomy at the same time that is sets commerce and industry free from the guardianship which the towns have hitherto imposed upon them. The protectionism and the exclusiveness of the bourgeoisies are brought to an end. If the craft-guilds continue to exist, yet they no longer control the organization of labor. New industries appear, which, to escape the meddling surveillance of the municipal authorities, establish themselves in the country. Side by side with the old privileged towns, which merely vegetate, younger manufacturing centres, full of strength and exuberance, arise; in England, Sheffield, and Birmingham, in Flanders, Hondschoote and Armentières.[28]

The spirit in which is now manifested in the world of business, is that same spirit of freedom which animates the intellectual world. In a society in process of formation, the individual, enfranchised, gives the rein to his boldness. He despises tradition, gives himself up with unrestrained delight to his virtuosity. There are to be no more limits on speculation, no more fetters on commerce, no more meddling of authority in relations between employers and employed. The most skillful wins. Competition, up to this time held in check, runs riot. In a few years enormous fortunes are built up, others are swallowed up in resounding bankruptcies. The Antwerp exchange is a pandemonium where bankers, deep-sea sailors, stock-jobbers, dealers in futures, millionaire merchants, jostle each other—and sharpers and adventurers to whom all means of money-getting, even assassination, are acceptable.

This confused recasting of the economic world transfers the rôle played by the capitalists of the late Middle Ages in a class of new[20] men. Few are the descendants of the business men of the fourteenth century among those of the fifteenth and sixteenth. Thrown out of their course by the current of events, they have not been willing to risk fortunes already acquired. Most of them are seen turning toward administrative careers, entering the service of the state as members of the councils of justice or finance and aspiring to the *noblesse de robe*, which, with the aid of fortunate marriages, will land their sons in the circle of the true nobility. As for the new rich of the period, they almost all appear to us like parvenus. Jacques Cœur is a parvenu in France. The Fugger and many other German financiers—the Herwarts, the Seilers, the Manlichs, the Haugs—are parvenus of whose families we know little before the fifteenth century, and so are the Frescobaldi and the Gualterotti of Florence, or that Gaspar Ducci of Pistoia who is perhaps the most representative of the fortune-hunters of the period.[29] Later, when Amsterdam has inherited the commercial hegemony of Antwerp, the importance of the parvenus characterizes it not less clearly. We may merely mention here, among the first makers of its greatness, Willem Usselinx,[30] Balthazar de Moucheron, Isaac Lemaire. And if from the world of commerce we turn toward that of industry the aspect is the same. Christophe Plantin, the famous printer, is the son of a simple peasant of Touraine.

The exuberance of capitalism which reached its height in the second half of the sixteenth century was not maintained. Even as the regulative spirit characteristic of the urban economy followed upon the freedom of the twelfth century, so mercantilism imposed itself upon commerce and industry in the seventeenth and eighteenth centuries. By protective duties and bounties on exportation, by subsidies of all sorts to manufactures and national navigation, by the acquiring of transmarine colonies, by the creation of privileged commercial companies, by the inspection of manufacturing processes, by the perfecting of means of transportation and the suppression of interior custom-houses, every state strives to increase its means of production, to close its market to its competitors, and to make the balance of trade incline in its favor. Doubtless the idea that "liberty is the soul of commerce" does not wholly disappear, but the endeavor is to regulate that liberty henceforward in conformity to the interest of the public weal. It is put under the control of intendants, of consuls, of chambers of commerce. We are entering into the period of national economy.

This was destined to last, as is familiar, until the moment when, in England at the end of the eighteenth century, on the Continent in[21] the first years of the nineteenth, the invention of machinery and the application of steam to manufacturing completely disorganized the conditions of economic activity. The phenomena of the sixteenth century are reproduced, but with tenfold intensity. Merchants accustomed to the routine of mercantilism and to state protection are pushed aside. We do not see them pushing forward into the career which opens itself before them, unless as lenders of money. In their turn, and as we have seen it at each great crisis of economic history, they retire from business and transform themselves into an aristocracy. Of the powerful houses which are established on all hands and which give the impetus to the modern industries of metallurgy, of the spinning and weaving of wool, linen, and cotton, hardly one is connected with the establishments existing before the end of the eighteenth century. Once again, it is new men, enterprising spirits, and sturdy characters which profit by the circumstances.[31] At most, the old capitalists, transformed into landed proprietors, play still an active rôle in the exploitation of the mines, because of the necessary dependence of that industry upon the possessors of the soil, but it can be safely affirmed that those who have presided over the gigantic progress of international economy, of the exuberant activity which now affects the whole world, were, as at the time of the Renaissance, parvenus, self-made men. As at the time of the Renaissance, again, their belief is in individualism and liberalism alone. Breaking with the traditions of the old régime, they take for their motto "*laissez faire, laissez passer*". They carry the consequences of the principle to an extreme. Unrestrained competition sets them to struggling with each other and soon arouses resistance in the form of socialism, among the proletariate that they are exploiting. And at the same time that that resistance arises to confront capital, the latter, itself suffering from the abuses of that freedom which had enabled it to rise, compels itself to discipline its affairs. Cartels, trusts, syndicates of producers, are organized, while states, perceiving that it is impossible to leave employers and employees longer to contend in anarchy, elaborate a social legislation; and international regulations, transcending the frontiers of the various countries, begin to be applied to working men.

I am aware how incomplete is this rapid sketch of the evolution of capitalism through a thousand years of history. As I said at the[22] beginning, I present it merely as an hypothesis resting on the very imperfect knowledge which we yet possess of the different movements of economic development. Yet, in so far as it is exact, it justifies the observation I made at the beginning of this study. It shows that the growth of capitalism is not a movement proceeding along a straight line, but has been marked, rather, by a series of separate impulses not forming continuations one of another, but interrupted by crises.

To this first remark may be added two others, which are in a way corollaries.

The first relates to the truly surprising regularity with which the phases of economic freedom and of economic regulation have succeeded each other. The free expansion of wandering commerce comes to its end in the urban economy, the individualistic ardor of the Renaissance leads to mercantilism, and finally, to the age of liberalism succeeds our own epoch of social legislation.

The second remark, with which I shall close, lies in the moral and political rather than the economic field. It may be stated in this form, that every class of capitalists is at the beginning animated by a clearly progressive and innovating spirit but becomes conservative as its activities become regulated. To convince one's self of this truth it is sufficient to recall that the merchants of the eleventh and twelfth centuries are the ancestors of the bourgeoisie and the creators of the first urban institutions; that the business men of the Renaissance struggled as energetically as the humanists against the social traditions of the Middle Ages; and finally, that those of the nineteenth century have been among the most ardent upholders of liberalism. This would suffice to prove to us, if we did not know it otherwise, that all these have at the beginning been nothing else than parvenus brought into action by the transformations of society, embarrassed neither by custom nor by routine, having nothing to lose and therefore the bolder in their race toward profit. But soon the primitive energy relaxes. The descendants of the new rich wish to preserve the situation which they have acquired, provided public authority will guarantee it to them, even at the price of a troublesome surveillance; they do not hesitate to place their influence at its service, and wait for the moment when, pushed aside by new men, they shall demand of the state that it recognize officially the rank to which they have raised their families, shall on their entrance into the nobility become a legal class and no longer a social group, and shall consider it beneath them to carry on that commerce which in the beginning made their fortunes.

FOOTNOTES:

[1] This article represents the substance of an address delivered at the International Congress of Historical Studies held in London, April, 1913.

[2] First edition in 1893.

[3] *Der Moderne Capitalismus* (1902).

[4] R. Heynen, *Zur Entstehung des Capitalismus in Venedig* (1905).

[5] H. Sieveking, "Die Capitalistische Entwickelung in den Italienischen Städten des Mittelalters", *Vierteljahrschrift für Social- und Wirtschaftsgeschichte* (1909).

[6] Davidsohn, *Forschungen zur Geschichte von Florenz*, III. 36; A. Doren, *Die Florentiner Wollentuchindustrie*, p. 481.

[7] A. Schaube, "Die Wollausfuhr Englands von 1272", *Vierteljahrschrift für Social- und Wirtschaftsgeschichte* (1908), pp. 39 ff. *Cf.* F. Keutgen, "Hansische Handelsgesellschaften", *ibid.* (1906), pp. 288 ff.

[8] *Cf.* H. Pirenne, *Les Anciennes Democraties des Pays-Bas*, pp. 11 ff.

[9] I. Goll, "Samo und die Karantinischen Slaven", *Mitteilungen des Instituts für Oesterreichische Geschichtsforschung*, vol. XI.

[10] A. Dopsch, *Die Wirtschaftsentwickelung der Karolingerzeit*, II. 274. I cannot, however, accept the thesis of Mr. Dopsch on the importance of commerce in the Carolingian period. The extremely interesting texts which he has assembled seem to me to establish the existence of a sporadic commerce only.

[11] Of course all the new towns did not grow up around an episcopal residence. Many of them, especially in the North and particularly in the Low Countries, had as their primitive nucleus a fortress (Ghent, Bruges, Ypres, Lille, Douai, etc.). But my purpose here is merely to recall the broad outlines of the subject.

[12] See on this subject the interesting article by W. Vogel, "Ein Seefahrender Kaufmann um 1100", *Hansische Geschichtsblätter* (1912), pp. 239 ff.

[13] "Unde non agriculturae delegit exercitia colere, sed potius, quae sagacioris animi sunt, rudimenta studuit arripiendo exercere."

[14] One finds already in the twelfth century lenders of money undertaking veritable financial operations. See H. Jenkinson and M. T. Stead, "William

Cade: a Financier of the Twelfth Century", *English Historical Review* (1913), p. 209 ff.

[15] *Die drei Bevölkerungsstufen.*

[16] The *Livre de la Vingtaine d'Arras* (ed. A. Guesnon) says, in speaking of the merchants of that town, in 1222, "Emunt non ad usum civitatis, sed ut exportent et discurrant per nondinas longinquas et per Lombardiam".

[17] G. von Below, "Grosshändler und Kleinhändler im Deutschen Mittelalter", *Jahrbücher für Nationalökonomie und Statistik* (1900).

[18] A. Schaube, "Die Wollausfuhr Englands vom Jahre 1273", *Vierteljahrschrift für Social- und Wirtschaftsgeschichte* (1908), p. 183.

[19] A. Duchesne, *Histoire des Maisons de Guines, d'Ardres et de Gand*, p. 289.

[20] Rymer, *Foedera*, vol. II., part IV., p. 49.

[21] For an example, see Espinas and Pirenne, *Recueil de Documents relatifs à l'Histoire de la Draperie Flamande*, II. 391.

[22] J. Kulischer, "Warenhändler und Geldausleiher im Mittelalter", *Zeitschrift für Volkswirtschaft*, etc., XVII. (1908).

[23] G. Espinas, "Jehan Boine-Broke, Bourgeois et Drapier Douaisien", *Vierteljahrschrift für Social- und Wirtschaftsgeschichte* (1904), pp. 34 ff.

[24] For the relations of the capitalists with the English crown see: Whitwell, "Italian Bankers and the English Crown", *Transactions of the Royal Historical Society*, XVII. (1903); and Bond, "Extract from the Liberate Rolls relative to the Loans supplied by Italian Merchants to the Kings of England", *Archaeologia*, XXVII. (1840). *Cf.* Hansen, "Der Englische Staatscredit unter König Edward III. und die Hansischen Kaufleute", *Hansische Geschichtsblätter* (1910).

[25] F. Arens, "Wilhelm Servat von Cahors als Kaufmann zu London", *Vierteljahrschrift für Social- und Wirtschaftsgeschichte* (1913), pp. 477 ff.

[26] V. Fris, "Thomas Fin, Receveur de Flandre", *Bulletin de la Commission Royale d'Histoire de Belgique* (1900), pp. 8 ff.

[27] Schneider, "Die Finanziellen Beziehungen der Florentinischen Banquiers zur Kirche", *Schmollers Forschungen*, vol. XVII.

[28] Pirenne, "Une Crise Industrielle an XVIe Siècle", *Bulletin de l'Académie Royale de Belgique*, classe des lettres (1905).

[29] R. Ehrenberg, *Das Zeitalter der Fugger*, I. 311 ff.

[30] J. F. Jameson, "Willem Usselinx", in Am. Hist. Assoc., *Papers*, II.

[31] See, in Cunningham, *The Growth of English Industry and Commerce in Modern Times*, p. 618, this citation from P. Gaskell: "Few of the men who entered the trade rich were successful. They trusted too much to others, too little to themselves." Let us recall here that the founder of the largest industrial establishments of Belgium, John Cockerill, was a simple workman. See E. Mahaim, "Les Débuts de l'Établissement John Cockerill à Seraing", *Vierteljahrschrift für Social- und Wirtschaftsgeschichte* (1905), p. 627.

Milton Keynes UK
Ingram Content Group UK Ltd.
UKHW030002260824
447288UK00004B/208